Know your spiritual gifts

Know your spiritual gifts

Bob Eckhard

Know your spiritual gifts

ISBN: 978-0-9556795-1-3

Creevagh Books, 4 Grosvenor Rd, London W7 1HJ

For further information on how to order additional copies of
this book, please visit the primary gift website:
www.primarygift.co.uk

(This book is printed on recycled paper)

Contents

Introduction 7

Notes to the reader 9

Primary gifts 11

Formational gifts 27

Passion and preference 35

Supernatural gifts 47

Creative gifts 51

What about evangelism? 57

Introduction

This book is intended as a resource for leaders and individuals keen to realise the full potential of their churches.

Back in 2004, I travelled to Chicago for a teaching and preaching conference at Willow Creek Church. The opening address by Bill Hybels was on the spiritual gifts God has given believers for building up the church. In particular, the understanding that every believer possesses a unique gift for service to the Church – a 'primary gift' that stands out from other gifts s/he might use.

Suffice to say, the talk was so inspiring, I knew then my understanding of church ministry would never be the same again. Three days later, I left the conference with the sense I had been privy to something special – a deep spiritual truth had been imparted to me, which was my responsibility to make available to others.

Returning to the UK, I re-read Selwyn Hughes book '*Discovering your place in the body of Christ*' in an attempt to provide a framework for understanding the basic spiritual gifts (Romans 12:6–8) within this new insight. For many years, problems remained as to how secondary and tertiary spiritual gifts should be understood within this model. However, after quite a bit of reflective thought, I think I may have arrived at an explanation as to the formational and ministerial benefit that occurs as these gifts are used.

A few years ago, I hosted a meeting for life group leaders at the church – an eclectic mix of people who braved a cold autumn evening to attend. Among them was Rosie – one of the worship leaders at the church, who also led a life group with her husband.

Turning to me in the coffee break, Rosie started enthusing about the need to get people into small groups where they could get excited by God's word and mature in their faith. Her comments surprised me because it was like listening to myself.

All of a sudden it hit me – KERBAM! Rosie's primary gift was not leading worship – it was teaching! The conversation that followed confirmed this as Rosie explained how she had been asked to help out with worship, but studying God's word was her real passion.

A couple of months later, Rosie gave her first sermon at the church and received nothing but praise. People approached me to ask why I had never asked her to do it before: her preaching was that good! Since then, Rosie has preached many sermons and is currently training at theological college as a reader in the Anglican Church.

She loves it. Why? Because her primary gift has been identified and she is now doing the thing God has given her to do in the Church.

Regrettably, many people in the church remain blissfully unaware of their primary gift. Usually, this is due to the fact that church members have received little or no teaching on this subject and have learnt to be content by 'helping out' in whatever way they can. Other times, the opportunity to place someone in the right position may be lost as ministers – desperate for anyone willing to fill a vacant ministry – may choose people without thought as to whether this is their primary gift or calling.

Although each of us is called to engage with and support a range of ministries within the church, problems begin to occur when assisting others replaces the thing God has designed for us to do. When that happens, spiritual malaise is quick to follow.

The first sign this is happening is often a sense of dissatisfaction or uneasiness about the ministry we are involved in. It may also be accompanied by a lack of energy and interest for the work. Returning home feeling exhausted every Sunday, we may even begin to feel aggrieved at the church leadership who have asked us to endure such things. Soon, Sunday has become a chore with no end in sight.

What to do?

Read this book - understand the differences between primary and formational gifts and the time you should be allocating to each. Complete the questionnaires and tasks to discern who you are and what God has gifted you to do. Then pray about the things you feel passionate about. The things God has laid on your heart and how you might use your primary gift to effect or enhance a related ministry in your church.

I believe that discovering God's equipping, calling and plan is the best thing a believer will ever do. Why? Because it fills each person with a great sense of satisfaction, but more importantly, it maximises the potential for the members of the Church to effectively minister in the world. This is my hope and prayer for you.

May God bless you richly as you discover the main thing you should be doing in God's church and excel at it. All the best!

Notes to the reader

Firstly, I make no claim that I have all the answers about spiritual gifts. The size and length of this book should tell you that further reading around the subject is advisable for those seeking more detailed understanding – particularly in regard to the supernatural gifts (1 Corinthians 12).

Secondly, there does not seem to be much material written on the subject of basic spiritual gifts. Even less so, the subject of primary gifts – which is staggering at a time when realising the full potential of human resources in the Church is a priority.

Although Willow Creek has produced church-based materials on spiritual gifts (The 'Network Course') I feel that people will benefit from a simplified resource that allows them to research and discover their primary gift for themselves. Hence, this book which is handy-sized and (hopefully) easy to read/use. Moreover, a book that follows the KISS principle of 'Keep It Simple, Stupid'.

Fourthly, I am human. I make mistakes. Ask anyone who has proofread for me or listened to one of my sermons. While I have endeavoured to devise questions that provide accurate outcomes, some will be poorly worded and may cause rogue results. Fear not, the Holy Spirit will not let God's purposes be thwarted by a misplaced tick or a question you left out because you were left baffled and perplexed.

Lastly, it is possible the content of this book will be problematic for some who believe (with Selwyn Hughes) that the spiritual gifts detailed in Romans 12 and Ephesians 4 are different and should never be grouped together. Although I have some sympathy with the idea about the 'gifts we receive' (Romans 12) and the 'gifts we become' (Ephesians 4), my intention is to provide a genus of basic gifts operating within the Church. Admittedly, some gifts and ministries are more common than others. For example, my experience tells me that prophets and apostles are a rare breed – rather like AB negative blood donors. However, helping people to understand the gifts they have been given (or have been using for years) will inevitably facilitate more people discovering their true calling in God's Kingdom plan. Something that has to be good news for the Church!

Primary gifts

Primary gifts

In 2004, I attended a conference in which Bill Hybels spoke about a period where Willow Creek Church grew numerically, but he was left feeling depressed and exhausted. Disillusioned with church activity, he sought a counsellor who was unable to help. Eventually, he worked out for himself what the problem was...

He had stopped using his primary gifting.

Bill Hybels continued by listing his gift set in priority order. These were:

1. **Leadership**   *(primary gift)*

2. **Evangelism**   *(secondary gift)*

3. **Teaching**   *(tertiary gift)*

Now, anyone who has heard Bill Hybels speak will know he is a great teacher. However, as the church grew, he was encouraged to take on more of a teaching role with the result that he spent less and less time using his primary gift of leading others. And this is what he came to realise about his gifts and the time spent using them. The gift we use determines whether our energy level is replenished or not.

So our...

Primary gift will *energise us*.

Secondary gift may *sustain us in the short term*.

Tertiary gift when continually used will *dissipate energy and exhaust us*.

As a result, when we do ministry outside of our primary gift, we soon tire and become disillusioned. (This was also Selwyn Hughes' experience). All of which means we have a responsibility to ensure we set aside time to facilitate activities that enable us to operate in our primary gift so that we renew our energy.

Although the Willow Creek conference happened a long time ago, I remember a suggestion that 65–70% of time be dedicated to ministry in activities connected to our primary gifting. Suffice to say this figure is not found anywhere in scripture. Moreover, the reality of life in a busy church may mean that things will arise where such an allocation of time becomes unfeasible or impractical. However, I believe the suggested figure serves more as a safeguard to ensure a reasonable amount of time is allocated to our main ministry area. Indeed, setting aside 65% of our time might only result in 51% of it being used for our primary gifting. Though last time I checked 51% was still the majority share.

Okay, so rounding up these figures, let's say the basic recommendation is that:

70% of time be spent using our primary gift.

30% of time is spent serving/using other gifts.
(The 30% will be addressed in the next chapter).

Gifts

In Romans 12:6–8, Ephesians 4:11 and 1 Corinthians 12:28, the apostle Paul lists the gifts God gives for the building up of the Church that are given to every believer at spiritual conversion. Namely:

preaching, serving, teaching, encouraging, generous giving, leading, pastoring, prophesy, evangelising, administrating and apostle

The scriptures suggest basic gifts are distributed throughout the Church and that every person has one gift that is particular to them – a primary gift. This is not to say the other basic gifts we possess are in any way redundant but rather we each possess a gift that will be uniquely significant when put to work in the way God is directing us.

With this in mind, complete the basic gift questionnaire on the following pages and the grid table to ascertain your three highest scoring gifts.

Basic gifts questionnaire

For each of the statements below, rate yourself using the following marking system:

True = 3
Sometimes true = 2
Seldom true = 1
Untrue = 0

Next to each question, assign a score that describes you best. For example if the first question never applies to you, give it a zero. If its totally you, give it a 3.

When you have finished scoring all of the statements, turn to page 19 and enter your scores onto the table. Then follow the instructions to sum total the scores for each basic gift to find the three basic gifts that are most akin to you.

1. When talking about God my explanations are enthusiastic and inspiring.
2. I invite people round for meals and look forward to entertaining.
3. I get excited when studying scripture and often see connections within it.
4. I am sometimes moved by a scripture, vision or word and feel compelled to share it with others in Church.
5. I often encourage people experiencing a crisis of faith.
6. I long for God to direct me to go out and plant a church.
7. I am financially secure and give generously to the church in one (or more) ways.
8. I have no problem delegating and releasing people into different areas of ministry.

9. I have empathy for people who have experienced a misfortune and readily sympathise with them.

10. I relish opportunities to meet others and tell them about Jesus.

11. I feel called to facilitate others by ensuring they are organised and adequate resourced.

12. I sense God is speaking through me as I challenge people to examine their spiritual life and motivation.

13. I am always ready to overlook my own personal comfort to help other people with their needs.

14. I delight in helping people to understand scripture so they might know how it applies to their life.

15. The spiritual revelations I receive from God motivate me to pass them on to others.

16. My desire is to see people spiritually mature and realise their full potential.

17. I desire to travel and reach out to every community – regardless of denomination – so Christ can be known everywhere.

18. I enjoy giving generously to the Church so the work of God may be advanced.

19. I get energised when supervising others and motivating them towards spiritual achievement.

20. I am keen to visit housebound people or those in hospital.

21. My idea of a great holiday involves meeting people and explaining why God loves them.

22. I believe the way a church becomes effective is where planning and guidance informs decision-making.

23. When speaking about God, my arguments are persuasive and may lead some people to be convicted about sin.

24. I feel most fulfilled when I am helping out around Church.

25. I feel strongly the Bible should be read and explained with accuracy of context.

26. Words from God are often experienced deeply in my heart mind and spirit.

27. I feel called to minister to people who are spiritually wounded.

28. Once a new church is established, I am keen to start another.

29. My financial situation allows me to give over and above that which others might contribute to the Church.

30. I sense God has called me to lead the community at this time.

31. I have deep concern for those who are in trouble and experiencing difficulty.

32. The prospect of leading someone to Christ excites me even at the risk of possible rejection.

33. I plan, advise and facilitate others as they work at their tasks in the church.

34. It is my intention when talking to people that it should finish with them being challenged to change in some way.

35. I enjoy serving coffees, welcoming people, attending church work parties hosting events and other such activities.

36. I consult books/commentaries so that I understand scripture and use correct terminology and vocabulary.

37. I feel led to speak out the word of God to the Church to challenge and/or encourage the congregation.

38. God often directs me towards people who need counselling.

39. I constantly seek new ways of making Christ known.

40. I am aware of situations that require money and will fund new initiatives without being asked.

41. I am not afraid to make tough decisions at cost to myself to protect the community of believers.

42. I regularly spend time talking with people who are ignored or isolated within Church.

43. I believe that more people should be involved in evangelistic activities.

44. I feel the need to set up and oversee systems in Church that help people become effective/efficient in doing their jobs.

45. When I talk with people, it helps them understand what is necessary for change in future.

46. I consider it an honour to help someone with their workload if it allows them the time to concentrate their effort on finishing a particular ministry task.

47. I work hard to understand scripture so that I can explain complex ideas in a simple way that is accessible to all.

48. Sometimes the word I receive from God is a message to more than one Church and my desire is that all should hear it.

49. I am acutely aware of the things that hinder people's spiritual growth and long to help them overcome these issues.

50. I will act in whatever way is necessary in order that the Church might grow and Christ be known everywhere.

51. I am careful with my finances so that I can extend my giving to the Church.

52. I am able to determine the way forward for the church and have the ability to inspire others to follow.

53. I share what others are going through and I am always ready to help when asked.

54. I do not hesitate when an opportunity occurs for me to share my faith with others.

55. I believe that where a Church organises, audits and utilises its resources carefully, it is one step closer to realising its full potential.

Basic gift table

Now that you have completed the questionnaire, transfer the marks you assigned for each statement onto the table (below). For example if you gave statement 1 a score of '3', insert that score in the top left-hand box, then the score for statement 2 in the box next to it, and so on until the table is complete.

	A	B	C	D	E	F	G	H	I	J	K
	1	2	3	4	5	6	7	8	9	10	11
	12	13	14	15	16	17	18	19	12	21	22
	23	24	25	26	27	28	29	30	31	32	33
	34	35	36	37	38	39	40	41	42	43	44
	45	46	47	48	49	50	51	52	53	54	55
Total											

When you have placed a score in each box of the table, sum total the rows vertically under the capital letter to work out your score for each column. For example A = 1 +12+23+34+45.

Write the total score against the appropriate column letter (on the next page) and repeat the process for each column. Identify your top three scores (possibly four) and mark them on the table overleaf. Then look at the gift profiles on pages 21–23 to see if these concur with who you are and what you presently do in church?

Column scores	Corresponding gift
A = ………	Preacher
B = ………	Server
C = ………	Teacher
D = ………	Prophet
E = ………	Encourager
F = ………	Apostle
G = ………	Generous giver
H = ………	Leader
I = ………	Pastor
J = ………	Evangelist
K = ………	Administrator

	Top Gifts	Score
1		
2		
3		
4		

Note: although a gift may score highly, it could be a secondary/tertiary gift - see page 23

Gift profiles

The following descriptions serve as a guide to understanding the roles and responsibilities of Church in present day context.

A. Preacher
People with the gift of preaching speak about God in an inspired and authoritative way. Always keen to address individuals, groups or congregations, they will convince and convict people through their arguments.

B. Server
People with this gift have a willingness to serve. They do not need to be asked twice to help and very often have no desire to be in a position of leadership over others. Whatever is asked of them, they do. Servers are the backbone of the Church and a real blessing to others.

C. Teacher
People with this gift are able to frame complex ideas in ways that make it easy for others to understand. They enjoy reading and discovering new things in the Bible and desire that others find these hidden treasures too. They need no coaxing to prepare sermons or study and will often be frustrated when others miss salient points in scripture that they consider obvious.

D. Prophet
A distinction exists between those who exercise a prophetic gift (1 Corinthians 12) and the rare few who have a prophetic role (Ephesians 4:11). Prophets are conduits God uses to speak to the Church. When receiving a word or revelation, they are often burdened until such time as they are released to reveal it to the people. This is usually verbal but could also involve some sort of living metaphor (Hosea 1). Prophets are dedicated to prayer.

E. Encourager

Encouragers possess good interpersonal skills and are people-focused. Nurturing and supportive, their focus is usually on counselling and prayer as this is what they do best. Their advice and encouragement is often inspired, recollecting passages, verses and other examples they consider helpful. They are always eager to see people mature and fulfil the potential that God has for them.

F. Apostle

Apostles pioneer new initiatives. They desire that everyone might know and experience Christ. Like prophets, they are a rare breed and are goal orientated in their decision-making.

G. Generous giver

These believers – sometimes entrepreneurial – are financially secure in ways that enable them to give generously to the work of the Church. As stewards of God's resources, there is nothing they enjoy more than supporting church projects, charitable organisations or individuals in need. Such giving may involve time, talent and/or money.

H. Leader

Although the gift of leadership may operate at a range of levels, some people clearly recognise it as their responsibility to lead and develop others. These leaders cast vision and inspire/motivate others with their plans. In team situations, they bring wisdom, insight and direction to whatever project is being undertaken.

I. Pastor

Those with the gift of sympathy (Romans 12:6–8) make good pastors. They spend time with people who are struggling or upset, and notice when a person is not at church. They possess empathetic skills and will utilise a variety of ways of contacting people through visiting, phoning, sending cards, enquiring through others, etc. Pastors are a listening ear, friendly face and concerned prayer.

J. Evangelist

Evangelists see every activity as an opportunity to tell someone about Jesus – no time or activity is off limits. Those with a speaking ministry are often productive and it is not unusual for people to respond to Christ as a result of their message combined with the Holy Spirit's conviction.

K. Administrator

These people oversee, guide and direct the effective use of human and financial resources within the church. This may involve activities in which they organise people in ministries, plan budgets and finance, or ensure adequate resources are available for church events. Without them, church flounders for lack of system and structure.

Identifying your primary gift

Having read through the gift profiles, consider the following that will help you determine which of the three/four gifts you listed is your primary gift.

1. **Which of these gifts energises you most?**

2. **When using this gift, are people blessed or edified?**

3. **Is there a sense of personal and spiritual fulfilment when operating in this gift?**

Okay, write your primary gift here:

....

Do not worry if you are unsure – the important thing is to use your gifts and monitor yourself over the next few weeks as to questions 1–3 above.

The 70/30 split

The box below has been divided into 70% and 30% areas. In the 70% section write down your primary gift.

In the 30% section, write down the other ten basic spiritual gifts from the list (though it's unlikely that 'apostle' or 'prophet will be a secondary gift for most people).

```
70% – Primary gift




















30% – Secondary formational gifts
```

If it helps, you might like to write '7 hours' and '3 hours' in the respective areas, imagining it as a 10-hour segment of time spent in service. Anything that gives you an idea of how much time you currently spend at church and on what type of activities.

Now, answer these two questions – space is provided below to write short answers.

1. Am I currently setting aside an adequate percentage of my time to use my primary gift?

    ....

2. What must I do (or stop doing) so that my primary gift is used more effectively?

    ....

    ....

Sometimes, people's natural ability as managers, doctors, teachers, nurses, musicians, finds an outlet in areas of church ministry. This 'talent' – useful as it is – may sometimes be mistaken as a primary gift in that the person appears very able and proficient. However, a person's primary gift is best measured by the outcomes it produces in terms of how it:

- develops, sustains, or advances the work of the church

- energises and motivates the person.

My primary gift is teaching. When I lead a bible study or teach in church, I often go home thoroughly energised. Indeed, it's not unusual for me to stay up late as I often need a couple of hours to calm down before going to bed.

In a different way, my friend Tim (who is an evangelist) loves nothing more than telling people about Jesus. Going on a cycle holiday with him, I struggle to get him out of the shops we call into because he is always talking and praying for someone.

I am not an evangelist like Tim. Likewise, he is not a teacher like me. Imagine how ineffective the church would be if I was the evangelist and Tim was the teacher. Hence, we each need to know our primary gift and how and where to use it. Which raises a different question…

How do we understand the parameters of Church?

It is clear from scripture that although Jesus' routine involved him worshipping God in synagogue and temple, the majority of his time was spent outside of these places as he met and engaged with needy people where they lived and worked. The gospels are full of instances of him speaking to outcasts (John 4:1–31, Luke 17:12–13), meeting real needs by intervening (John 8:3–11), teaching others (John 3:1–21, Matthew 6) and healing people (Luke 7:1–16, John 9:1–11). However, more interesting than the dealings with adulterous women, grieving widows, lepers and fearful leaders is that it all occurs outside of the established religious premises where we might imagine it would happen. In short, Jesus refuses to allow his ministry to be confined within religious structures and buildings.

We too need to have the same attitude and outlook as Jesus by working hard to ensure that our use of spiritual gifts does not become constrained to activities that occur on church premises. Only then, will we model him and engage fully with the community around us. Whether that's showing hospitality in church, at home or in the soup kitchen. Telling someone about Jesus at work, in the supermarket or as part of a Sunday school lesson. Encouraging friends, neighbours or the recently bereaved person at church. These are the ways our spiritual gifts should be used to reach out beyond the church premises we visit (for a fraction of our week) so that our full spiritual potential is realised. Enough said – don't hide behind a pew. Engage with the world!

Formational gifts

Formational gifts

In the previous chapter we considered the importance of identifying our primary gift and allocating it 70% of our time. We also recognised that in a busy church, operating in our ministry area for 51% of our time would be an achievement in itself. Next, we turn our attention to what happens with the remainder of our time. The hours and minutes when we are not occupied using our primary gift.

Ideally, if we are very disciplined in our division of ministry, the time available to each of us should be somewhere between 30–49%. Time where we help out with ministry inside and outside church. Everything from cleaning the premises to making the tea; planning the barbeque to counselling/praying for a friend; preparing a bible study to visiting someone in hospital; teaching in Sunday school to giving someone a lift home afterwards. Sacrificial acts offered to the body of Christ because we are grateful that Jesus Christ sacrificed himself for us. Moreover, we recognise that we are now part of God's family and have a responsibility to love one another if we are truly Christ's disciples (John 13:35).

These activities and ministries I have chosen to group together and call 'formational gifts'.

> It will be helpful at this point to turn back to page 24 and look again at the table labelled 'primary and 'formational gifts.'

You will see that aside from your primary gift, every other gift is formational.

The reason is that because our *primary gift* excites, motivates and energises us, it costs very little to engage emotionally, mentally, physically and spiritually in these activities. We know what we are doing and it's a real pleasure.

Conversely, *formational gifts* will dissipate energy from us when we use them over a prolonged period of time. This is because helping others in a way that requires sacrifice is not akin to how we normally think and act. We find it hard to put others before ourselves – but when we do, something changes within us as we are transformed in our thinking. As we 'choose' to sacrifice so we begin to engage in a process of change. That is why these gifts and activities are best described as 'formational'.

My primary gift is teaching. If someone asks me to teach a course at church, no one has to force me to do it. I am immediately on board – ready, willing and able. However, if I arrive at church the following day and discover no one has put out chairs for the service then it's a different matter because this now requires sacrifice on my part. I am not energised or enthused by the thought of putting out 200 chairs by myself. Before I can set out the chairs I first have to overcome my self-centred desires that would cause me to avoid the task and not sacrifice myself for my brothers and sisters.

Naturally, we often view activity that holds little or no interest for us, as something we need to complete in order to get on with the thing we would rather be doing. However, when we engage in acts of sacrificial ministry, something transformational happens – we create an opportunity for Christ to be formed in us through our response to the act of service. When we elect to participate, so we align our heart with God, allowing Christ to permeate our lives and mould our attitude and actions – serving others because they are spiritual brothers and sisters, equally valued and loved by the Father.

What does it mean in practice?

Well, if your primary gift is pastor, you love to go out and visit the sick and housebound. However, when you secretly drop an envelope of money through someone's door that is sacrificial and an opportunity for more of Christ to be formed in you.

Likewise, if your primary gift is generosity, there is nothing you will like better than to devote your time, talent or money to the church. Yet when you agree to prepare the bible study because the leader is off sick then something formational happens as God works in your heart of sacrifice and service.

Similarly, if your primary gift is teaching children about Jesus, you don't dread Sunday – you love it. You can't wait to see their smiling faces. But when you stay behind after the children have gone and help wash cups in the kitchen, then transformation occurs as Christ meets you in that act of service.

Maybe your primary gift is serving. You jump at the opportunity of giving someone a lift home or opening up the church for a wedding. But when you forego your favourite programme on television to attend the Church prayer meeting because it is important to do so, then Christ is formed in you.

To summarise, formational gifts are where we avail ourselves to the opportunity of serving others in a way that is outside our comfort zone and/or natural disposition. As we engage in these sorts of activities, something transformational happens within us. More than that – it happens in the church! Because we no longer do it for the reason that it's enjoyable. We do it because it is what Jesus requires us to do as an act of obedient sacrifice in service to others.

With this in mind, it will be helpful to say something here about consumer culture. Today, it is easy for people to get seduced into the trap of engaging only with the ministries they enjoy doing. Indeed, I know a worship leader who, when asked if he would lend a hand serving refreshments after the service, explained that he couldn't do it because
'it wasn't his ministry'.

His mistake was a failure to understand that Jesus requires us to be transformed in our heart and minds through acts of service towards others. All of which means…

If your primary gift is evangelism and a church member turns to you this Sunday with tears in their eyes, you may be called upon to perform the ministry of a pastor. Likewise, if you are a pastor and the church administrator asks you to help place letters in envelopes, then this will be a useful task for you to do.

Why?

- it is an act of love towards the person

- it serves Christ and his church

- it transforms us in ways that enables the likeness of Christ to be made manifest.

Basically, it is done out of love for Jesus because you want to help the person – in the same way that you might hope if the situations were reversed, the person would do the same for you (Mark 12:31).

> Now complete the following assignment designed to help you understand and identify the various tasks that might come your way and whether they are primary or formational activities for you.

Primary or formational activities?

Now that you know your primary gift, write beside each statement whether the activity is formational (F) or primary (P) for you.

1. You visit someone who is sick.

2. You post money through the door of a family who cannot pay their bills.

3. You help out with Sunday School for a term.

4. You agree to lead a bible study.

5. You go around your area inviting people to the local church mission.

6. You make a meal and take it round to someone who's ill.

7. You agree to lead youth ministry while the leader is away on maternity leave.

8. You give up your time to help someone complete a tax form.

9. You produce a budget to monitor church expenditure.

10. You meet someone after church who is struggling with faith and stay behind to listen, talk and pray with them.

11. You sense God has given you a word for the church and you take it to leadership.

12. You discover the church toilets are blocked and deal with it.

13. You turn to the person sitting next to you on the bus and explain to them why they should accept Jesus Christ.

14. You learn that an elderly person is about to be thrown out of their house and call round to see how you might help.

15. You respond to a prompting from God, to give sacrificially and fund a project.

16. You sort out a rota allocating leaders to children's groups.

17. The youth leader asks you to give your testimony to the teenagers to explain why they should accept Christ.

18. You attend the prayer meeting (trick question!).

19. You serve in the kitchen preparing food for the church Christmas meal.

20. You sign up for a mission overseas where the plan is to help build a hospital for sick children.

21. You coordinate and lead an event in the community.

22. You counsel someone after church.

23. You agree to bank money for the church each week.

Passion and preference

Passion and preference

Having established our primary gift (Chapter 1) and the way in which we serve in formational ministry (Chapter 2), we now consider who we are and what we bring to a team.

In this section we will consider the ways that personality colours and affects our participation in church activity. I need to say that I am not a psychologist and what is offered here is gleaned from my reading of books around this subject. Anyone wanting an accurate assessment of their personality and preferences should seek a trained professional who can administer a psychometric test such as Myer-Briggs or Belbin.

We are all created in God's image and yet each of us is a unique representation of God that will never be repeated. When Christ comes to live within each person (through the Holy Spirit) he uses our gifts, talents, temperament and personality to reveal God's love to others. Actually, this should not come as a surprise as we are different from one another. That is why some people are drawn to us but others are not. Likewise, we know that others will befriend people we find difficult to get on with. It is part of the diversity we share as the collected community of Christ.

Although we are different, there are ways in which we are similar and share the same needs. For example, we all crave (to greater or lesser degrees) community. We all need rest, food and exercise. We enjoy social interaction, music and entertainment – though we may disagree as to what is enjoyable, funny or artistically pleasing. It is just how we are.

For many years I considered myself extrovert. I am naturally sociable and have no qualms about approaching new people. Indeed, before discovering my own primary gift, I headed up hospitality and welcome at a church for eight years. Aside from the fact I spent a good few years outside my primary gifting, I discovered something very important about myself: namely, after a day of chatting and engaging with people, I was worn out and ready to retreat somewhere by myself to recharge. Something I now understand as behaviour more characteristic of a gregarious introvert!

Psychological dynamics and intricacies aside what I present next is a very simplistic way of identifying between an extrovert and introvert (as some understand it):

Extroverts recharge by being around people

However,

Introverts recharge by being alone

John Donne famously coined the phrase 'No man is an island', because he understood that we are created for community with one another. Yet, a mix of personality, preference and upbringing determines the degree to which we seek others out for company. Many introverts are happy living alone for weeks on end while some extroverts feel a day by themselves is unbearable.

I mention this because we all need to be:
'aware of who we are and how we function.'

But more importantly we must:
'know the types of activity that will tire us.'

That is why an extrovert who gets energised by talking to people, finds a 24-hour silent retreat hard work. Likewise, the introvert who goes away to camp with the youth group is going to be worn out by the end of it. Not that any of us are excused from doing these activities – it's part of our formational gifting (30%), but it's good to understand what we're doing and how it is not always akin to our natural leaning and personality. With this in mind, ask yourself now:

'Am I extrovert or introvert?'

'Do I get energy by being around or away from people?'

Reflect on the activities you currently do and the amount of contact you have with people.

Focus orientation

Tick the statements that you are in agreement with.

1) Better to return a phone call once the job you're doing is finished.

2) Paperwork gets in the way of ministering to people.

3) I prefer to finish an assignment rather than take a break and lose my train of thought.

4) The church is about serving people and not about planning.

5) Life would be a lot easier if people sorted themselves out.

6) It is good to spend time listening to people and praying for them.

7) I'd rather work alone on a project then have people trying to help.

8) A phone call is a welcome distraction from work.

9) Things must be organised effectively.

10) We engage with God when we engage with people.

Goal orientated or people person?

Look again at the statements you ticked. Although it is not an accurate test, a majority of ticks placed against:

Even numbers suggests you are **people focused**.

Odd numbers suggest you are **goal orientated.**

Goal-orientated people enjoy working in isolation and may be frustrated by interruptions that require them to deal with problems not related to the goal. People's problems may be seen as obstacles that have to be dealt with so they can get back to the thing that really matters.

Those in church who are **people focused** are usually happy spending their day engaging with a range of people. They enjoy talking with people and are happy to help in whatever way they can.

Now, somewhere between these two positions sit a range of people who are a mix of the two – possibly through personality, training, upbringing, or all three. However, the important thing to understand here is how our disposition towards people or projects, determines:

1. Our suitability for the activities we do

2. The expectations we make of others

3. The safeguards we have for ourselves.

Where do I fit?

Read the statements below, and put **one** tick (per box) beside the statement you identify with most.

1.

a)	I am keen to see areas of church ministry developed and improved.
b)	I am keen to serve and help others in church.

2.

a)	I am passionate about changing the way we do church.
b)	I am passionate about meeting with people and serving in whatever way I can.

3.

a)	I get excited thinking about how God will progress the life and ministry of the Church.
b)	I get excited thinking about how God is using the church at this present time.

4.

a)	I love to enthuse people about where we are going and what we are trying to achieve.
b)	I love to help out in whatever way I can.

5.

a)	The church needs to plan for change and reinvent itself.
b)	The church needs to remind people of the value of service to others.

Look at the statements you have ticked.

If you ticked mainly category 'a' statements, you are more likely a visionary – in which case go to p43 and read the visionary profile.

If you have ticked mainly category 'b' you are either an enabler or a sustainer – in which case, complete the additional questions (below).

1.

c) I am most happy when a new ministry gets off the ground.

d) I am most happy when I am serving others.

2.

c) I work best when I help others find their ministry in church.

d) I work best when someone takes responsibility for ministry.

3.

c) My attitude is that I am there to do a job for a fixed period.

d) My attitude is that I am in it for the long haul.

4.

c) I facilitate others by ensuring that the ministry happens.

d) I facilitate others by a willingness to serve them in whatever way I can.

5.

c) It is most important to support a new ministry in the first six months to a year.

d) It is most important to support a new ministry faithfully in the years after it is established.

Again, there are more detailed questionnaires with ways of eliciting more accurate answers. However, as a rough guide…

- A majority of ticks in category 'c' suggests you are best suited as an enabler in the church.

- A majority of ticks in category 'd' suggests you are best suited as a sustainer of ministry.

- If you have a range of letters a, c and d, you will have to deduce from trial and error which role suits you best.

The 3 types of people necessary for every church ministry are:

Visionaries – Enablers – Sustainers

Visionaries are goal-orientated people who are full of ideas. They are not people focused as 'goal' is important to them. Once a project is up and running they may get itchy feet and want to progress onto another idea as they have no interest in leading it long-term.

Enablers catch the vision for a project and facilitate it by motivating others to get involved. They provide a link between the visionary and those who will eventually sustain the project when it is up and running. They bring a range of different skills that are necessary for the project to get off the ground.

Sustainers are passionate about the ministry and will continue to faithfully serve in it because it connects with their primary gift and calling.

What are you passionate about?

In the same way that God equips us with a range of spiritual gifts, he also gives us a passion for certain issues and groups of people. This is how one person ends up teaching children in church while another goes off to work with adult disciples. Both have the same spiritual gift – teaching. What separates them is their passion.

This is why it is important to identify the groups and issues you are passionate about. Because using the right primary gifting with the wrong group of people or issue can be as ineffective and unfulfilling as not knowing your spiritual gift at all. Now, complete the questionnaire 'What am I passionate about?'

Tick every box that applies to you. Ask yourself: Does this sort of group or ministry excite and motivate me? (NOTE: There are no right or wrong answers – just what you are passionate about)

Part 1
What sort of people are you passionate about serving?

   a) Families?

   b) Women?

   c) Men?

   d) Singles?

   e) Elderly?

   f) Children?

   g) Crèche?

   h) Teenagers?

   i) Those outside of church?

   j) Single parents?

   k) Orphans?

   l) .... (Group not on the list? Write it here.)

Part 2

What sort of ministry are you passionate about?

a) Making disciples?

b) Evangelism?

c) Preaching or teaching?

d) Hospitality?

e) Being good news in the community?

f) Serving others?

g) Welcoming people?

h) Giving generously?

i) Administrative skills and/or leadership?

j) Pastoring people?

k) Social action?

l) Mission abroad?

m) Something else? Please state ....

Now write down all the things you feel strongly about inside church and outside, in the wider community:

Supernatural gifts

Supernatural gifts

This will be a short chapter for two reasons: first, there are hundreds of books on this subject by people more qualified than me. Second, my intention is to identify the value of supernatural gifts (listed in 1 Corinthians 12) as it 'fits' within the context of primary and formational ministry.

Selwyn Hughes observes that although God *'gives'* basic gifts (Romans 12:6–8 and Ephesians 4:11) to each believer, we are all encouraged to *'seek'* supernatural gifts. In other words, there is no limit on the number of supernatural gifts God may place at our disposal. Interestingly, Hughes also observed his supernatural gift often dovetailed in with his primary gift of preaching and recounts how prophetic words of knowledge would come to him while giving sermons.

This mixing of the supernatural and primary is echoed in Paul's observation to the Corinthians (1Corinthians 12:7) where he notes…

'to each is given a manifestation of the Spirit for the common good'

Moreover, Paul makes no attempt to delineate between gifts akin to our natural ability and those ascertained though prayer and the laying on of hands. Indeed, in the verses that follow, the primary gifts of 'teaching, helping and administrating' are listed amongst supernatural gifts of 'speaking in tongues' and 'prophesy', which suggests he sees all as God-given and integral to one another.

Often, in my own ministry of teaching, a scripture verse will sometimes come to mind while I am speaking or ministering to people in prayer afterwards. Other times I have a strong sense about a person's motivation and the degree to which they are passionate about God or more focused on other things that are operating in their life. Insights that at times can and do direct the content of what I discuss and/or pray with them later on.

Naturally, the instruction to 'earnestly seek' supernatural gifts should be viewed with as much importance and priority as identifying our primary ministry and passion. To not engage with the process of personal renewal and supernatural equipping is to spiritually hamstring ourselves by limiting the way God can work through us.

When teaching this material to churches and groups as a course, I always allocate one session to understanding and using supernatural gifts. A practical session where – after a brief introduction to 1 Corinthian 12 – I encourage people to stand and take turns praying for one another. For many, this is a moving experience as the Holy Spirit comes and inspires them to pray words of encouragement, commendation, prophetical utterance and affirmation. An experience that is often as beneficial to the group praying as it is to the person receiving as they realise God is using them in this way.

If you know the supernatural gifts God has given you, write them down now in the space beneath.

If you have never received prayer for supernatural equipping, may I encourage you to read 1 Corinthians 12 then ask your church leader or someone else you trust (in whom these gifts operate) to pray for you.

Creative gifts

Creative gifts

These gifts are well documented throughout scripture. Everything from the embroidery of priestly garments to the architecture of the temple is referenced in the Bible. Indeed, the world owes a huge debt of gratitude to people who, inspired by God over the centuries, have produced beautiful works of art, composed music, written verse and constructed buildings in praise of the Creator of all things.

There is no doubt that some people are particularly creative. They have a natural talent and/or disposition for artistic things from birth. Others require years of study and training to develop the necessary skills. Whatever way people come to develop their skill, it is the calling of God upon their life that will eventually determine how the gift is used and what will follow.

Of course, in a different way, all of us can be creative for God in our work – whether we are artistic or not. The book of Genesis (1:26) informs us we are made in the image of our Creator. Although people understand this verse in a variety of ways, I believe that one aspect is that humans have a capacity to think and act creatively. The multitude and scope of things built, composed, designed, written, drawn, etc. suggests that being creative is very much a part of who we are. However, unlike God who is a primary Creator (creating everything from nothing), humans are secondary creators in that we work from the resources he has placed at our disposal.

So, what does this mean for us?

Personally, I believe we are called to be creative in everything we do – whether we are at home, working, resting or attending Church. For example, we can creatively reorder our living room or garden. Or plan a holiday that inspires adults and teenage children alike (bordering on the impossible, but it can be done!). We can try out new methods for teaching children who are struggling to learn or suggest different ways that problems in the workplace can be managed. We can try out new leisure activities in an attempt to relax and unwind. And lastly, we can bring our creative ways of thinking to the different ministries we are involved in at Church – particularly when it is connected to the use of our primary gift.

Just recently, I was teaching the last two sessions on the Alpha course. One of the talks was 'How do I get filled with the Holy Spirit?'

Preparing the session, I thought it would be useful to use a jug of water to demonstrate what happens to us when we ask the Holy Spirit to fill us. Initially, my thinking was to submerge a sponge to show how the Holy Spirit saturates us. However, as the day drew closer, a different idea came to mind.

Re-reading Roy Hession's book *'Be filled now'*, I was drawn to the section where he details three attitudes to the Holy Spirit by which people may grieve, quench or resist what God is trying to do. In a flash, it came to me! Grip the sponge so tight so that no water is taken into it when placed in the jug.

The day arrived and I performed my demonstration. The sponge came out as dry as it went in. I asked the group why it had not taken water and one person immediately answered: 'you didn't release your grip'. I went on to explain that our soul is like a sponge and the different attitudes and hang-ups we have, will determine the degree to which God is allowed access. For good measure, I began to release each finger noting how one 'quenches', another 'grieves', a third 'resists' and the fourth majors on 'unbelief'.

Later that day, a few people shared how they had found the demonstration helpful, telling me they had not seen anything like it before. Now, I am not so naive to think it was an original idea, as I believe the Holy Spirit will have inspired others to do the same demonstration somewhere else. The reason I tell the story is to show how God makes us creative through the inspiration and prompting of the Holy Spirit to do things differently. Maybe an idea about how people might be better welcomed or networked into church? Or how the church accounts might be presented in a way that helps people to understand the figures, or give more generously? Or possibly an idea to rethink the way people are effectively pastored in church? Or an inspirational word or verse that could come to mind as you are counselling or praying for someone. Other examples of creative activity might involve the management and distribution of refreshments to people after church? Or making people aware of poverty and fair trade issues in the developing world.

Whatever our ministry, God calls us to be creative as we serve one another, using both our primary and formational gifting.

What about evangelism?

What about evangelism?

A year after becoming a Christian, I got involved with a beach mission to foreign students in Bournemouth. However, it soon became evident to me that I was reluctant to press people into conversations about Jesus. My own journey to discovering Christ had been rather gentle and it felt alien to force the conversation.

Returning to university, I dutifully helped with 'door to door' mission on campus and around the estate where my church was located. My motivation was the Great Commission (Matthew 28) as I sensed people needed to know about Jesus.

In the years that followed, I discovered that while I felt compelled to tell people about Jesus, I would only do this in situations where the conversation arose naturally. To my surprise, this method worked better for me and I found myself engaging with friends and other people in a way that did not feel like I had somehow 'forced' the discussion upon them.

Particularly helpful at this time was a quote attributed to St Francis of Assisi who instructs:

'Preach the gospel at all times and if necessary use words.'

Now, I do not want to put shackles on any evangelists reading this because I believe missionaries are God's gift to the Church and do invaluable work. However, God has equipped and gifted them specifically for this task. Evangelists like nothing better than going out for the day with the hope they will meet someone and have an opportunity to tell them about Jesus. But for the rest of us, we know we are not like that! And hopefully you too will know by now if this is or isn't your primary gifting.

Does this excuse us from engaging with people and telling them about Jesus? No – it is part of our formational gifting. The salient warning about being embarrassed or fearful over owning Jesus Christ as Saviour and Lord, applies as much to us today as it did in the first century.

**'If a person is ashamed of me and my message, then I will be.
ashamed of that person when I return in my glory and in the
glory of the Father and the holy angels.'** *Luke 9:26*

So how should we evangelise?

My own thinking on this, and the reason I believe the gift of
evangelist is omitted from the list in Romans 12:6–8, is that all of us
are expected to engage in acts of evangelism. How we do it is a
different matter.

Here, I can only speak from my own experience. In the same way that
the foot cannot be an eye, nor the nose an ear, we are created and
placed in the body of Christ for different purposes. That said, I think
we each have a responsibility to play our part in explaining and
showing Christ's love to those around us who presently do not know
him.

I have always found the model that JF Engel produced very helpful in
understanding the journey that people take in which they move from
no knowledge of God through to the point of conversion and
complete maturity in Christ. A series of steps that each takes in their
journey towards knowing God, which we are expected to participate
in by answering questions, explaining scripture, showing love,
patience, kindness, grace, etc. Of course, it often is an evangelist who
leads them to Christ, but we each have a part to play in cooperating
with the Holy Spirit as he moves people closer towards the point of
understanding/commitment.

Earlier in the book, I mentioned how I served on a welcome team for
many years. Often, this presented me with opportunities to talk to
people who knew little or nothing about God. Reflecting back, many
of these discussions involved me explaining and opening up scripture
- which is of course my primary gift. Which leaves me wondering if
our primary gift provides the key to how we are most naturally
equipped to talk to others about the good news of Jesus Christ.

For some people, this is the faithful and friendly serving of others with cups of tea, plates of food, or spotlessly clean toilets – activities that reveal the love of Christ in ways that speak louder than any well rehearsed anecdote or memory verse. Or perhaps it is the woman with the gift of encouragement who explains something in such a way that it helps the person take a step closer to God. Or maybe a man who responds to a prompting from the Holy Spirit to post some money through the door of a neighbour, and unwittingly answers the person's prayer to God. Or the pastor who diligently visits someone in hospital and becomes the tangible presence of Christ to the person he serves.

It seems to me that evangelism is often made harder than it needs to be. Sometimes this occurs from pressure we place on ourselves. Other times it is guilt heaped on us from the preaching evangelist who advocates that we should all be like him or her, not realising the diversity of primary gifts and what the body would look like if we were all a foot.

The best we can do is pray that God will lead us across the paths of those people he is reaching out to and give us wisdom and discernment about how we should speak and reveal Christ to them.

Amen.

Appendix 1: Summary table

It may be useful to record information that you gathered from the various questionnaires throughout this book in the table below.

Primary gift (p23)	
Formational gifts (p24)	
Extrovert/introvert (p38)	
People focused/goal orientated (p39)	
Visionary/enabler/sustainer (p43)	
Supernatural gifts? (p50)	
Passions – people + ministries (p44–45)	

(You might want to copy this list out and hand it to your church leader so he or she will know your gift set and how you might serve most effectively).